EMMANUEL JOSEPH

Crypto Odyssey: Trading in the Age of Digital Currency

Copyright © 2025 by Emmanuel Joseph

All rights reserved. No part of this publication may be reproduced, stored or transmitted in any form or by any means, electronic, mechanical, photocopying, recording, scanning, or otherwise without written permission from the publisher. It is illegal to copy this book, post it to a website, or distribute it by any other means without permission.

First edition

*This book was professionally typeset on Reedsy.
Find out more at reedsy.com*

Contents

1	Chapter 1: The Dawn of Digital Currency	1
2	Chapter 2: Navigating the Crypto Market	3
3	Chapter 3: The Role of Blockchain Technology	5
4	Chapter 4: The Rise of Decentralized Finance (DeFi)	7
5	Chapter 5: The Intersection of Cryptocurrencies and...	9
6	Chapter 6: The Future of Digital Payments	11
7	Chapter 7: Legal and Regulatory Challenges	13
8	Chapter 8: Security and Privacy in the Crypto World	15
9	Chapter 9: The Environmental Impact of Cryptocurrencies	17
10	Chapter 10: The Social Impact of Cryptocurrencies	19
11	Chapter 11: The Evolution of Crypto Communities	21
12	Chapter 12: The Road Ahead for Digital Currencies	23

1

Chapter 1: The Dawn of Digital Currency

In the early 21st century, the financial world witnessed an unprecedented revolution with the advent of digital currencies. Bitcoin, the first decentralized cryptocurrency, emerged in 2009, created by the mysterious figure Satoshi Nakamoto. This marked the beginning of a new era where traditional financial systems were challenged by the concept of a peer-to-peer electronic cash system. Digital currencies promised lower transaction fees, enhanced security, and the possibility of financial inclusion for millions of unbanked individuals worldwide.

As Bitcoin gained popularity, a multitude of other cryptocurrencies began to emerge, each with unique features and use cases. Ethereum introduced the concept of smart contracts, allowing developers to create decentralized applications on its blockchain. Meanwhile, Litecoin, Ripple, and other altcoins offered various improvements in transaction speed and scalability. The proliferation of these digital assets sparked interest from tech enthusiasts, investors, and even governments, leading to a global discourse on the future of money.

The rise of digital currencies also brought with it numerous challenges and controversies. Regulatory bodies around the world grappled with how to categorize and manage these new assets. Issues such as price volatility, security breaches, and the potential for money laundering and fraud became focal points of debate. Despite these hurdles, the adoption of digital currencies continued to grow, fueled by a growing belief in their potential to reshape the financial landscape.

By the mid-2020s, the digital currency market had matured significantly. Major financial institutions began to incorporate cryptocurrencies into their portfolios, and central banks explored the possibility of issuing their own digital currencies. The stage was set for a new era of innovation and disruption in the financial world, with digital currencies at the forefront of this transformation.

2

Chapter 2: Navigating the Crypto Market

Entering the world of cryptocurrency trading can be both exciting and daunting for newcomers. The market's volatility and the plethora of available digital assets require traders to develop a solid understanding of the fundamentals. One of the first steps for any aspiring crypto trader is to familiarize themselves with the various types of cryptocurrencies and their underlying technologies. This knowledge forms the foundation for making informed investment decisions.

In addition to understanding the technical aspects of digital currencies, successful crypto traders must also develop a keen sense of market trends and sentiment. Various factors, such as regulatory news, technological advancements, and macroeconomic events, can significantly impact the price of cryptocurrencies. Traders must stay up-to-date with the latest developments and learn to analyze market data to anticipate potential price movements. Tools such as technical analysis and fundamental analysis can be invaluable in this regard.

Risk management is another crucial aspect of cryptocurrency trading. Given the market's inherent volatility, traders must be prepared for sudden price swings and potential losses. Implementing strategies such as setting stop-loss orders, diversifying investments, and maintaining a disciplined approach can help mitigate risks. Additionally, having a clear understanding of one's risk tolerance and investment goals is essential for long-term success in the crypto market.

As traders gain experience and confidence, they can explore more advanced trading strategies and techniques. Leveraging, short selling, and arbitrage are just a few examples of strategies that can potentially yield higher returns. However, these approaches also come with increased risks, and it is important for traders to thoroughly understand and carefully evaluate their suitability before incorporating them into their trading arsenal.

3

Chapter 3: The Role of Blockchain Technology

At the core of all digital currencies lies blockchain technology, a decentralized and immutable ledger that records all transactions. This groundbreaking innovation not only ensures the security and transparency of cryptocurrency transactions but also has far-reaching implications for various industries. Understanding how blockchain technology works is essential for grasping the true potential of digital currencies.

A blockchain is essentially a chain of blocks, each containing a list of transactions. These blocks are linked together using cryptographic hashes, creating a secure and tamper-proof record. The decentralized nature of blockchain means that no single entity has control over the entire network. Instead, transactions are validated by a network of nodes, which work together to maintain the integrity of the ledger. This consensus mechanism is a key feature that sets blockchain apart from traditional centralized systems.

One of the most significant advantages of blockchain technology is its ability to facilitate trustless transactions. In a blockchain network, parties can transact directly with one another without the need for intermediaries such as banks or payment processors. This not only reduces transaction costs but also eliminates the risk of fraud and censorship. The transparent nature of blockchain also ensures that all participants can verify the authenticity of transactions, further enhancing trust and security.

Beyond digital currencies, blockchain technology has the potential to revolutionize various sectors, including supply chain management, healthcare, and finance. By providing a secure and transparent way to track assets and verify information, blockchain can streamline processes, reduce costs, and improve efficiency. As the technology continues to evolve, we can expect to see an increasing number of innovative applications that leverage the power of blockchain to address real-world challenges.

4

Chapter 4: The Rise of Decentralized Finance (DeFi)

Decentralized Finance, or DeFi, is a rapidly growing movement that aims to create an open and permissionless financial system using blockchain technology. By leveraging smart contracts and decentralized protocols, DeFi platforms offer a wide range of financial services, including lending, borrowing, trading, and investing, without the need for traditional intermediaries. This has the potential to democratize access to financial services and empower individuals around the world.

One of the key components of DeFi is the use of smart contracts, which are self-executing agreements with the terms of the contract directly written into code. These contracts automatically execute transactions when predefined conditions are met, eliminating the need for intermediaries and reducing the risk of human error. DeFi platforms such as MakerDAO, Compound, and Uniswap have gained significant traction, offering users the ability to earn interest on their assets, take out loans, and trade digital currencies in a decentralized manner.

The rise of DeFi has also given birth to a new wave of financial innovation, with novel concepts such as yield farming, liquidity mining, and decentralized exchanges (DEXs) becoming increasingly popular. Yield farming involves providing liquidity to DeFi platforms in exchange for rewards, while liquidity mining incentivizes users to contribute to the liquidity pools of decentralized exchanges. These mechanisms not only provide users with additional earning opportunities but also contribute to the overall stability and liquidity of the DeFi ecosystem.

Despite its many advantages, the DeFi space is not without its challenges. Security vulnerabilities, regulatory uncertainty, and the potential for market manipulation are some of the risks associated with decentralized finance. As the DeFi ecosystem continues to grow and mature, it will be essential for developers, regulators, and users to work together to address these issues and ensure the long-term sustainability of this emerging financial paradigm.

5

Chapter 5: The Intersection of Cryptocurrencies and Traditional Finance

As digital currencies gain mainstream acceptance, the lines between cryptocurrencies and traditional finance are becoming increasingly blurred. Financial institutions, including banks, hedge funds, and asset managers, are beginning to recognize the potential of digital assets and are incorporating them into their portfolios. This convergence of traditional finance and cryptocurrencies is paving the way for a more integrated and inclusive financial system.

One of the most notable developments in this regard is the introduction of cryptocurrency exchange-traded funds (ETFs). These investment vehicles allow investors to gain exposure to digital currencies without having to directly purchase and store them. The approval of Bitcoin ETFs in various jurisdictions has been a significant milestone, attracting institutional investors and legitimizing digital assets as a viable asset class. As more cryptocurrency ETFs are introduced, we can expect to see increased participation from both retail and institutional investors.

Another area where cryptocurrencies are making inroads into traditional finance is through the development of central bank digital currencies (CBDCs). Several central banks, including those of China, Sweden, and the Bahamas, have already launched or are in the process of developing their own digital currencies. CBDCs aim to combine the benefits of digital currencies, such as faster and cheaper transactions, with the stability and trust associated with traditional fiat currencies. The widespread adoption of CBDCs could further accelerate the integration of digital currencies into the global financial system.

The growing acceptance of digital currencies by traditional financial institutions has also led to the emergence of new financial products and services. Cryptocurrency lending and borrowing platforms, digital asset custodians, and blockchain-based payment solutions are just a few examples of how the financial landscape is evolving. As the lines between cryptocurrencies and traditional finance continue to blur, we can expect to see an increasing number of innovative solutions that leverage the best of both worlds.

6

Chapter 6: The Future of Digital Payments

The rapid rise of digital currencies has the potential to transform the way we make payments. Traditional payment systems, which rely on intermediaries such as banks and payment processors, can be slow, costly, and prone to fraud. In contrast, digital currencies offer a faster, cheaper, and more secure alternative, making them an attractive option for both consumers and businesses.

One of the most significant advantages of digital currencies is their ability to facilitate cross-border payments. Traditional international transfers can take several days to process and incur high fees. Digital currencies, on the other hand, enable near-instantaneous cross-border transactions at a fraction of the cost. This has the potential to revolutionize remittances, enabling individuals to send money to their loved ones more quickly and affordably. Various blockchain-based payment platforms, such as Ripple and Stellar, are already making strides in this area, offering efficient and low-cost solutions for cross-border payments.

The adoption of digital currencies for everyday transactions is also on the rise. With the increasing availability of cryptocurrency payment gateways and point-of-sale systems, businesses are beginning to accept digital currencies as a form of payment. This is particularly evident in the e-commerce sector, where the integration of cryptocurrency payment options is becoming more common. As more merchants embrace digital currencies, consumers will have greater flexibility and choice in how they make payments.

However, the widespread adoption of digital currencies for payments is not without its challenges. Issues such as price volatility, regulatory uncertainty, and the need for user-friendly interfaces must be addressed to be addressed to ensure that digital currencies can achieve mainstream adoption. For instance, stablecoins, which are digital currencies pegged to traditional assets like the US dollar, offer a potential solution to the issue of price volatility. By providing a more stable store of value, stablecoins can make digital payments more practical for everyday use. As regulatory frameworks evolve and technological advancements are made, the adoption of digital currencies for payments is expected to continue to grow, paving the way for a more efficient and inclusive global payment system.

7

Chapter 7: Legal and Regulatory Challenges

The rise of digital currencies has posed significant challenges for regulators and policymakers around the world. Cryptocurrencies operate in a decentralized and borderless manner, making it difficult for traditional regulatory frameworks to keep pace. Governments and regulatory bodies have had to grapple with issues such as consumer protection, anti-money laundering (AML) measures, tax implications, and the potential for market manipulation.

One of the primary concerns for regulators is the potential for cryptocurrencies to be used for illicit activities. The pseudonymous nature of digital currency transactions can make it difficult to trace the movement of funds, raising concerns about money laundering, terrorism financing, and other illegal activities. In response, many countries have implemented AML and Know Your Customer (KYC) regulations for cryptocurrency exchanges and other service providers to enhance transparency and accountability in the crypto space.

Taxation is another complex issue that regulators must address. The decentralized nature of cryptocurrencies makes it challenging to track and report transactions for tax purposes. Different countries have adopted various approaches to taxing digital assets, ranging from treating them as property to considering them as currency. As the adoption of cryptocurrencies continues to grow, it will be crucial for regulators to develop clear and consistent tax guidelines to ensure compliance and prevent tax evasion.

Despite these challenges, there has been significant progress in developing regulatory frameworks for digital currencies. Many countries have introduced comprehensive regulations to govern the use of cryptocurrencies, while others have established regulatory sandboxes to test new approaches in a controlled environment. The continued collaboration between regulators, industry stakeholders, and policymakers will be essential in creating a balanced regulatory landscape that fosters innovation while protecting consumers and maintaining financial stability.

8

Chapter 8: Security and Privacy in the Crypto World

Security and privacy are paramount concerns in the world of digital currencies. While blockchain technology offers robust security features, the crypto ecosystem is not immune to threats such as hacking, phishing, and fraud. Ensuring the safety of digital assets and protecting the privacy of users requires a multi-faceted approach that includes both technological solutions and best practices.

One of the most significant security risks in the crypto space is the potential for hacking attacks on exchanges and wallets. Over the years, there have been numerous high-profile incidents where hackers have stolen millions of dollars' worth of digital assets. To mitigate this risk, it is essential for users to choose reputable exchanges and wallet providers that implement strong security measures, such as multi-factor authentication, cold storage, and regular security audits.

Phishing attacks are another common threat in the crypto world. Cybercriminals often use deceptive emails, websites, and social media profiles to trick users into revealing their private keys or login credentials. To protect against phishing, users should be cautious when clicking on links, verify the authenticity of websites and communications, and never share their private keys with anyone.

Privacy is also a critical consideration for cryptocurrency users. While blockchain transactions are transparent and publicly accessible, they are pseudonymous, meaning that users' identities are not directly linked to their wallet addresses. However, sophisticated analysis techniques can sometimes be used to deanonymize transactions and trace them back to individuals. To enhance privacy, users can employ various techniques, such as using privacy-focused cryptocurrencies like Monero and Zcash, mixing services, and employing best practices for transaction management.

As the crypto ecosystem continues to evolve, ongoing efforts to improve security and privacy will be essential in building trust and confidence among users. By staying informed about the latest threats and adopting best practices, individuals can better protect their digital assets and enjoy a more secure and private experience in the world of cryptocurrencies.

9

Chapter 9: The Environmental Impact of Cryptocurrencies

The environmental impact of cryptocurrencies, particularly those that rely on proof-of-work (PoW) consensus mechanisms, has become a topic of increasing concern. Bitcoin mining, for example, requires significant computational power and energy consumption, leading to a substantial carbon footprint. As the popularity of digital currencies continues to grow, addressing their environmental impact is becoming a critical issue for the industry.

Bitcoin mining involves solving complex mathematical problems to validate transactions and secure the network. This process requires specialized hardware and consumes a large amount of electricity. Critics argue that the energy-intensive nature of PoW mining contributes to climate change and environmental degradation, particularly when the electricity used is derived from non-renewable sources.

In response to these concerns, various initiatives and technological advancements are being explored to reduce the environmental impact of cryptocurrencies. One such approach is the transition to more energy-efficient consensus mechanisms, such as proof-of-stake (PoS). Unlike PoW, PoS does not require miners to compete in solving mathematical problems. Instead, validators are chosen based on the number of coins they hold and are willing to "stake" as collateral. This significantly reduces the energy consumption associated with securing the network.

Several cryptocurrency projects have already adopted PoS or are in the process of transitioning to it. For instance, Ethereum, the second-largest cryptocurrency by market capitalization, is undergoing an upgrade known as Ethereum 2.0, which aims to shift from PoW to PoS. This transition is expected to significantly reduce Ethereum's energy consumption and improve its scalability.

In addition to adopting more sustainable consensus mechanisms, efforts are being made to power cryptocurrency mining operations with renewable energy sources. Some mining farms have relocated to regions with abundant renewable energy, such as hydropower, wind, and solar, to minimize their carbon footprint. By embracing green energy solutions, the crypto industry can mitigate its environmental impact and contribute to a more sustainable future.

10

Chapter 10: The Social Impact of Cryptocurrencies

Cryptocurrencies have the potential to drive significant social change by promoting financial inclusion and empowering individuals in underserved communities. Traditional financial systems often exclude large segments of the population due to factors such as lack of access to banking services, high transaction fees, and stringent regulatory requirements. Digital currencies, with their decentralized and borderless nature, offer an alternative that can bridge these gaps and create new opportunities for financial participation.

One of the most notable social impacts of cryptocurrencies is their ability to provide financial services to the unbanked and underbanked populations. In many developing countries, access to banking infrastructure is limited, making it difficult for individuals to save money, obtain loans, or participate in the global economy. Cryptocurrencies enable anyone with an internet connection to access a wide range of financial services, from digital wallets and remittance platforms to decentralized lending and borrowing protocols. This can help individuals build wealth, achieve economic stability, and improve their quality of life.

Cryptocurrencies also have the potential to reduce transaction costs and increase the efficiency of remittances. Millions of people around the world rely on remittances from family members working abroad to support their households. Traditional remittance services often charge high fees and take several days to process transactions. In contrast, digital currencies enable near-instantaneous cross-border transfers at a fraction of the cost, ensuring that more money reaches those who need it most.

Furthermore, the transparency and security provided by blockchain technology can help combat corruption and improve governance. By recording transactions on an immutable and publicly accessible ledger, blockchain can enhance accountability and reduce the potential for fraud and misuse of funds. This is particularly relevant in the context of charitable donations and humanitarian aid, where ensuring that funds are used effectively and reach their intended recipients is crucial.

As the adoption of cryptocurrencies continues to grow, their social impact will become increasingly apparent. By promoting financial inclusion, reducing transaction costs, and enhancing transparency, digital currencies have the potential to drive positive change and create a more equitable and inclusive global financial system.

11

Chapter 11: The Evolution of Crypto Communities

Crypto communities play a vital role in the development and adoption of digital currencies. These decentralized and often grassroots movements consist of enthusiasts, developers, investors, and advocates who collaborate to advance the technology, raise awareness, and drive innovation. The evolution of crypto communities has been instrumental in shaping the landscape of the cryptocurrency industry.

In the early days of Bitcoin, the crypto community was relatively small and primarily consisted of tech enthusiasts and libertarians who were drawn to the idea of a decentralized and censorship-resistant currency. Online forums and chat rooms, such as Bitcointalk and the Bitcoin subreddit, served as the primary platforms for discussion and collaboration. These early adopters played a crucial role in promoting Bitcoin and educating the public about its potential.

As the cryptocurrency ecosystem expanded, so did the diversity and complexity of crypto communities. The launch of Ethereum and its smart contract capabilities, for example, attracted a new wave of developers and entrepreneurs who saw the potential to build decentralized applications (DApps) and create new use cases for blockchain technology. This led to the formation of various project-specific communities, each with its own unique goals and vision.

Crypto communities have also been instrumental in driving the adoption of decentralized finance (DeFi) and non-fungible tokens (NFTs). These emerging sectors have garnered significant attention and participation from users worldwide, thanks in large part to the efforts of passionate community members. Social media platforms, online forums, and meetups have become essential tools for sharing knowledge, fostering collaboration, and building a sense of belonging among crypto enthusiasts.

The evolution of crypto communities has not been without its challenges. As the industry has grown, it has attracted a diverse range of participants, including institutional investors and mainstream media. This influx of new players has sometimes led to tensions and divisions within communities, as differing priorities and perspectives clash. However, the resilience and adaptability of crypto communities have enabled them to navigate these challenges and continue to drive innovation and progress.

As the cryptocurrency landscape continues to landscape continues to evolve, the role of crypto communities will remain vital. These decentralized networks of individuals have demonstrated their ability to drive innovation, advocate for adoption, and support one another in navigating the complexities of the crypto world. By fostering collaboration, sharing knowledge, and maintaining a strong sense of community, crypto enthusiasts can continue to shape the future of digital currencies.

12

Chapter 12: The Road Ahead for Digital Currencies

As we look to the future, it is clear that digital currencies will play an increasingly significant role in the global financial system. The rapid pace of technological advancements, coupled with growing acceptance and adoption, suggests that we are on the brink of a new financial paradigm. However, several key challenges and opportunities lie ahead as we navigate this uncharted territory.

One of the most pressing challenges is the need for regulatory clarity and consistency. As digital currencies continue to gain mainstream acceptance, it will be crucial for governments and regulatory bodies to develop comprehensive frameworks that balance innovation with consumer protection and financial stability. This will require ongoing collaboration and dialogue between industry stakeholders, policymakers, and regulators to ensure that the regulatory landscape evolves in a way that fosters growth and innovation.

Another key area of focus will be the development of scalable and sustainable technologies. As the demand for digital currencies grows, it is essential to address issues such as transaction speed, network congestion, and energy consumption. Innovations in consensus mechanisms, layer-two scaling solutions, and the integration of renewable energy sources can help ensure that digital currencies remain efficient, secure, and environmentally friendly.

The continued evolution of digital currencies will also bring about new opportunities for financial inclusion and economic empowerment. By providing access to financial services for underserved populations and reducing barriers to entry, digital currencies have the potential to create a more inclusive and equitable financial system. As we move forward, it will be important to prioritize initiatives that promote financial literacy, bridge the digital divide, and empower individuals to participate in the global economy.

In conclusion, the journey of digital currencies has been nothing short of a revolution, reshaping the financial landscape and challenging the status quo. As we continue to explore the possibilities and navigate the challenges, one thing is certain: the age of digital currency is here to stay. By embracing innovation, fostering collaboration, and addressing the critical issues that lie ahead, we can unlock the full potential of digital currencies and pave the way for a more inclusive, efficient, and sustainable financial future.

www.ingramcontent.com/pod-product-compliance
Lightning Source LLC
LaVergne TN
LVHW020743090526
838202LV00057BA/6199